11·14

I'M ALLERGIC TO MILK

Maria Nelson

Stevens

Please visit our website, www.garethstevens.com. For a free color catalog of all our high-quality books, call toll free 1-800-542-2595 or fax 1-877-542-2596.

Library of Congress Cataloging-in-Publication Data

Nelson, Maria.
I'm allergic to milk / by Maria Nelson.
 p. cm. — (I'm allergic)
Includes index.
ISBN 978-1-4824-0969-7 (pbk.)
ISBN 978-1-4824-0970-3 (6-pack)
ISBN 978-1-4824-0968-0 (library binding)
1. Food allergy — Juvenile literature. 2. Food allergy in children — Juvenile literature.
3. Milk — Juvenile literature. I. Nelson, Maria. II. Title.
RC596.N45 2014
616.97—d23

Published in 2015 by
Gareth Stevens Publishing
111 East 14th Street, Suite 349
New York, NY 10003

Copyright © 2015 Gareth Stevens Publishing

Designer: Nicholas Domiano
Editor: Kristen Rajczak

Photo credits: cover, p. 1 (face) © iStockphoto.com/princessdlaf; cover, p.1 (body) Blend Images/Thinkstock.com; pp. 3–24 (background texture) iStock/Thinkstock.com; p. 5 Paul/Getty Images; p. 7 amisb/Shutterstock.com; p. 9 Levent Konuk/Shutterstock.com; p. 11 Photodisc/Thinkstock.com; p. 13 Medic Image/Universal Images Group/Getty Images; p. 15 Sukharevskyy Dmytro/Shutterstock.com; p. 17 Peter Dazeley/Photographer's Choice/Getty Images; p. 19 Rus S/Shutterstock.com; p. 21 (label) alexmillos/Shutterstock.com; p. 21 (bottle) Winston Link/Shutterstock.com.

Printed in the United States of America

CPSIA compliance information: Batch #CS15GS: For further information contact Gareth Stevens, New York, New York at 1-800-542-2595.

CONTENTS

Boldface words appear in the glossary.

Got Milk?

Milk is a healthy addition to any meal. But some people can't eat or drink anything that has milk in it! They're allergic to milk. This means their body **reacts** badly to it.

Most allergic reactions to milk happen because the body has made antibodies against milk **proteins**. Antibodies are special parts of the blood. They fight germs and other matter the body thinks is an **intruder**.

What's a Reaction Like?

Allergic reactions can happen within a couple minutes or a few hours of taking in milk or milk products. Common allergic reactions to milk include **hives** and **swelling** around the mouth and eyes.

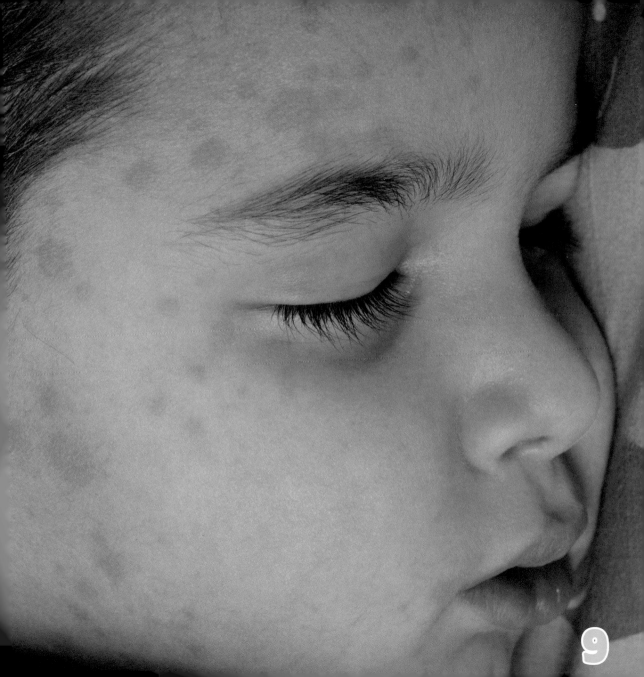

Milk allergies can cause you to have a tummy ache or throw up. Some people have trouble breathing and swallowing. If their throat closes up, they might pass out.

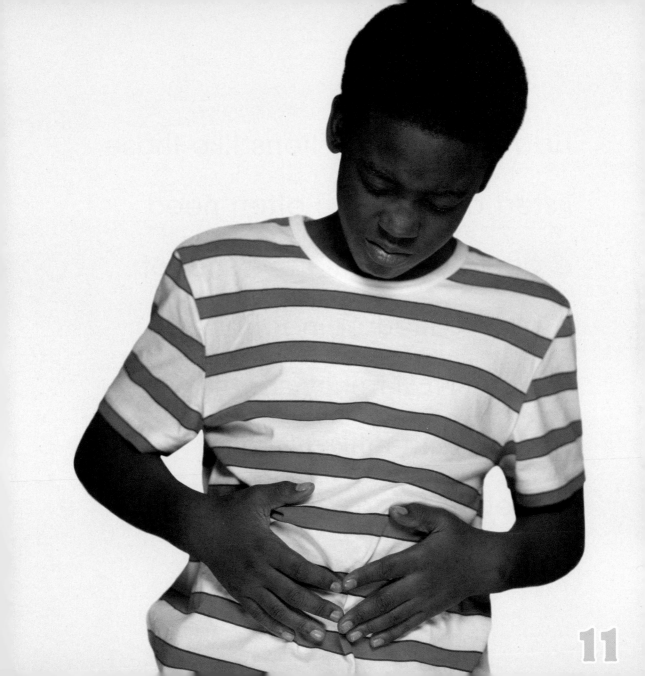

11

Bad allergic reactions like those listed on page 10 often need a doctor's attention. A shot of a drug called epinephrine (eh-puh-NEH-fruhn) can help. People with milk allergies sometimes carry their own shot, just in case.

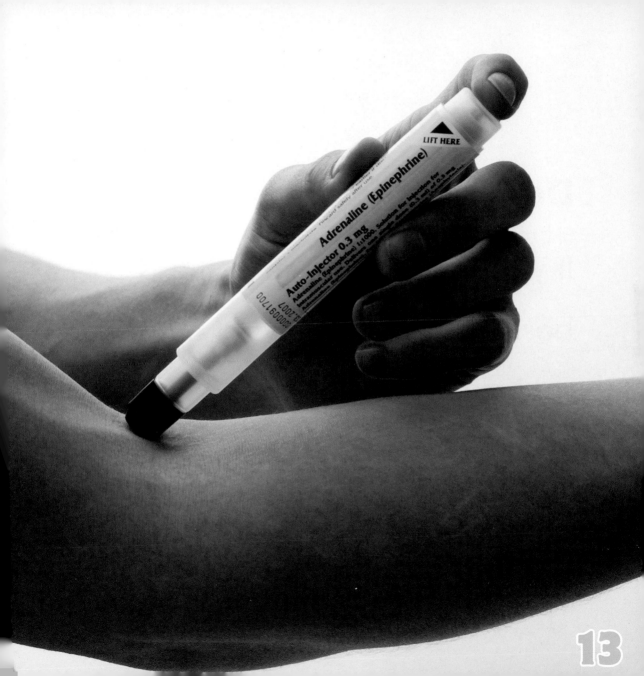

Don't Eat That

If you're allergic to milk, the best thing to do is **avoid** milk and milk products. That means you can't eat butter, ice cream, yogurt, or cheese.

When you have a milk allergy, you have to read food labels to make sure your food isn't made with milk. One word to look for is "casein." Casein is a milk protein that's often in a lot of products—even gum!

INGREDIENTS

Sugar . Wheatflour . Paste
Egg . Butter (10%) . Lem
Sunflower Oil . Low Fat
Vegetable Glycerine . P
Agent: E450, E501).

ALLERGY INFORMA

CONTAINS Milk, Eggs, Wheat,

Made in a factory that uses Nut in

17

Good News

Milk allergies are one of the most common in children. Luckily, many outgrow it by age 8. Most have outgrown the allergy by the time they're a teenager.

Lactose Intolerance

Some people's bodies can't break down a sugar called lactose found in milk. They're lactose intolerant. They may feel sick when they take in milk, but it's not the same as being allergic.

GLOSSARY

avoid: stay away from

hives: raised, itchy patches of skin that are redder or paler than the skin around them

intruder: someone who forces their way into a place they're not wanted

protein: one of the building blocks of food

react: respond

swelling: getting bigger in an uncommon way

BOOKS

Moragne, Wendy. *Allergies*. Minneapolis, MN: Twenty-First Century Books, 2012.

Wethington, Julie. *Yes I Can! Have My Cake and Food Allergies, Too*. Columbia, MD: DragonWing Books, 2012.

WEBSITES

Cooking Recipes Milk-Free and Dairy-Free
www.kidswithfoodallergies.org/resourcespre. php?id=103#recipes
Find ways to substitute dairy ingredients when cooking and follow cool dairy-free recipes.

Milk Allergy
kidshealth.org/teen/food_fitness/nutrition/milk_allergy.html
Learn more about what happens when you have a milk allergy and how to treat it.

INDEX